LETTING YOUR LIGHT SHINE

Inspiration and Quotations

*Believe More, Become More;
Allow Yourself to Stand in Your Own
Power and Let Your Light Shine*

DR. STEM SITHEMBILE MAHLATINI

LETTING YOUR LIGHT SHINE

Inspiration and Quotations

Believe More, Become More; Allow Yourself to Stand in Your Own Power and Let Your Light Shine

Copyright © 2022 Dr. Stem Sithembile Mahlatini.
All rights reserved.

ISBN 979-8-9864291-7-5

All rights reserved.
No part of this publication may be reproduced, stored in a retrieval system, or transmitted in any way by any means – electronic, mechanical, photocopy, recording, or otherwise – without the prior permissions of the copyright holder, except by reviewer who may quote brief passages in a review to be printed in magazine newspaper or by radio / TV announcement, as provided by USA copyright law. The author and the publisher will not be held responsible for any errors within the manuscript. All characters appearing in this work are _fictitious. Any resemblance to real persons, living or dead is purely coincidental.

Written by: Dr. Stem Sithembile Mahlatini

drstem14@gmail.com
www.drstemspeaks.com | www.drstemmie.com

Facebook: DrStem Mahlatini
Twitter: DrStemahlatini
LinkedIn: Drstem Mahlatini
Skype: Dr.Mahlatini

Foreword by: Dr.Stem Sithembile Mahlatini
Cover Design by: Simba Mukundinashe.

Category: Category: Motivational, Inspirational, Empowerment, Educational
and Empowerment

Printed in the USA

Foreword

This Life of Mine, I'm Gonna Make it Shine, Make it Shine, Make it Shine.

On Oct 24, 2018, I conjured the courage to go bald. Yes, I cut all my hair and decided to be Free and Fearless. A lot of people asked why? Some wondered why, but I knew that this bald move was unexplainable.

However, I know why. I was tired of just talking and not moving my life and my work to the next level. I was tired of emotional holds, excuses, unexplained fears, and family values. I was tired!

I also had looked at the calendar and realized we only had two months to the end of 2018, and that was not settling well with me. I needed to promise myself that 2019 was not going to be another stagnant year filled with empty promises, wishes, and a bucket full of plans.

Although 2020 brought us all to a halt, stripping us of everything we knew, it was to me also a year of brevity and baldness. I saw many people young and old get out of their comfort zone and reveal strength that they did not even think they had. It was a time to get out of our comfort zones and become bald beyond our fears, values and beliefs.

Being bald has brought me to another level of baldness. I will now take even bigger risks and take my life to a level higher than I've ever dreamt. I now know being bald means change. Change is not easy. It is true you cannot expect to get different results being in the same place, doing the same things. You will have to change to get different results.

It isn't easy to make changes, but there's no better advice than this: just do your best. Make sure you stay strong enough to move ahead, because there are some wonderful rewards waiting for you when you get the courage to be bald. Not every change you will make will makes sense right away, but with time, you will definitely start to see answers, decisions will prove to be the right ones, and the path will become clearer.

Giving up has never been an option for me. I always tell people that my biggest risk was leaving my parents and siblings in Zimbabwe and embarking to the USA in 1986. After that, every other move and risk had to be taken to live the free and fearless life I came to seek.

My dream is to have enough money to go back and help those in Zimbabwe, build schools, hospitals, training schools and help those that want to start businesses or go to college. To do that, I have to have money, and to have money, I have to take even bigger risks. In my language shona we have this saying, " Shungu dzarwizi". Ask me in my live workshops to explain, because I will be meeting you soon, if you are reading this. We will absolutely meet and talk about your journey and my journey in one of the many workshops, conferences, seminars that God has prepared me for during this ONE LIFETIME of mine, to let my light shine.

I am so excited of the Women Empowerment Conference I started in 2020 titled "Bounce Back Empowerment Conference, which is held on the third Sat of December every year. Learn more on my website www.drstemmie.com

For three years since moving to Orlando, FL, I honestly thought I could never regain my energy, zeal and excitement of becoming the world renounced motivational speaker, workshop presenter, retreat coordinator, television and radio personality I have always wanted to be. But, today, I am digging my dusty dreams out of my own fears, known and unknown. I am Ready to Let My Light Shine and Help You Shine Your As Well. There is Room for All of Us and More. Are You Ready?

Let me tell you, I am ready, so ready I can't stop smiling and thanking God for this moment, this year 2022. The game has changed.

My vivid, complicated, detailed dreams are back. The running dialogue in my head as I live my life has returned, the big dreamer is dreaming big and acting boldly again. And, I must say, it feels really good and this time all the pieces are moving into place, all the pieces.

I know that I have the courage to be fearless. Will you follow along? When my confidence wavers, when I start to mumble, will you remind me fear is a measly four-letter word? Enjoy this guide to becoming a free and fearless you.

This encouraging book is a sign of my rebirth. It is the result of my new baldness and boldness. It is my way to help you become your best, as well. I know without a shadow of doubt that whatever I have been able to do, you can do it too, and more. I also know that what others have done, I too can do.

To my parents, Benjamin and Idah Mahlatini, thank you for giving me life. My siblings, nieces and nephews, I can only be and do the best me to lead you. Be your best and everything will work out. To all my supporters, followers and prayer warriors, may God open up doors for you like never before. Be Encouraged and Encouraging.

I look forward to hearing your story and how you were able to boldly make decisions and how you are able to let your own light shine and ignite that of others. Email me at drstem14@gmail.com if you would like me to interview you on my radio show The DrStem Show *"Be You Be Free Be Fearless"* Or Publish Your Book.

To be interviewed for my Radio/TV/Podcast Email me at drstemshow@gmail.com

You've Only got three choices in life:

Give Up, Give in or Give it all you've got!

Letting Your Light Shine

During this time of transition from the deadly pandemic, let us remember that there is a bigger purpose for each of us and God is not finished with us. Your job is to rewrite and retell your story and allow your light to shine. Yes it is time – Let Your Light Shine. Stop being afraid of yourself, Believe in Your Dream, Believe in Your Vision and Yes Believe in Your Passion. Let Your Life Shine.

The light is used symbolically and may be spiritually which means let your inner goodness and humanity shine through the darkness around the world. In today's life a lot of people lose hope and feel demotivated by stress and failure.

Spread the positive vibes and let your soul shine through all the evils in the world. This will help people around to be more hopeful, and will encourage them to live in peace, with love and courage.

If you're like me, you have learned the hard way that this world can be a scary and dark place. **Sometimes:** People are mean. Selfish. Abusive. Fake. Hard to figure out. *__Ignorant and insensitive to the pain of others.__* Deeply flawed.

But, you know what is even more scary? We can become a part of this list of *imperfect* people if we are not careful. Without proper care, we are capable of inflicting the same pain we experience upon the people around us. *Sigh* My thoughts at this moment are probably similar to yours,

"I don't want to continue the cycle of pain in the world. I don't want to foster on the impact and effects of covid19. I am taking back my power and life desires. I want to be a solution. I want to help end the pain."

You and I see the deep pain in the world, in others and we don't like it! Let us be different. Let us embrace the Power to Be The light, to show up with pure joy and gratitude each and every day to each and every person.

Women like you and I realize that while we are present on earth we have to make a change. After complaining and nursing our wounds; Then, we have to accept our true job titles as World Changers, We have to allow our own light to shine and help light that of others.

As World changers we are women that allow the light inside them of us to shine so bright that it removes the darkness in the world!

The truth is, if you care to make this world a better place, it starts with YOU. ***Yes, YOU!***

So, it's time to beautify yourself, your soul and your heart. It is time to allow yourself to go through a process of making your heart pure, healed, and beautiful.

I am here to help.

If you have not seen this program and enroll, this is one you want to check out. The Unleash the Real YOU Within - Become UNSTOPPABLE was designed with every woman in mind, it is a Coaching program focused on three key things... To have every woman who goes through it feel renewed, refreshed and replenished. Visit www.drstemmie.com or email me drstem14@gmail.com for link.

I strongly believe that if we *'let our hearts shine we can brighten up this dark world!'*

Dream with me for a second. **Imagine:** An army of empowered women with beautiful (adorned) hearts, littering the world like stars in the sky. Each woman, bringing the beauty within her which allows a light to shine into the darkest corners of humanity.

So, take the time to beautify your heart and fill it with kindness, humility, love, patience, selflessness, etc. The world needs people like you. People who are willing to fight the pain and embrace healing.

You are a woman that refuses to give the world what it deserves – evil for evil. **The world needs women like you that fight to be kind and considerate, despite the pain and live their life with nothing but pure joy and love.**

Here are a few quick steps of where you can begin

Learn To Love Yourself

This is the key step to totally embracing this unique creation that you are. I have personally learned that when we have a relationship with God and let him love us, we start to love ourselves. We are able to see ourselves clearly.

Remember: *Your* **beauty** *should not come from outward* **adornment** *such as braided hair or gold jewelry or fine clothes,* **but from the inner disposition of your heart,** *the unfading beauty of a gentle and quiet* *spirit, which is precious in God's sight. For this is how the holy women of the past adorned themselves.* — ***1 Peter 3:3-5***

To Learn More about Our Easy To Follow Video and Audio Self Love Program please visit our websites:

www.drstemmie.com *or*
www.womenempowermentworkshops.com

Learn To Love Others

Relationships with others are supposed to be fun and amazing! However due to internal struggles people don't know how to deal with their own pain and the pain of others. As we learn to love ourselves we can learn to have relationships with others in a healthy way.

Let your heart so shine so bright that Heaven sees it and smiles! Fulfill the calling of the let your light shine quotes and bible verses you will find in this book.

If you are a believer Let God Love You: Allow God To Heal Your Pain

Allowing God to love you is a part of having a relationship with him. He wants to heal you and make your life better. He gives guidelines in the Bible to help us live a good life. For instance, he says love forgives because he knows how un-forgiveness can damage you and your relationships. Every advice or command given from God is from love. He knows if you take advice opposite of the Bible it will invite problems in your life.

I have leaned that I am not able to navigate this dark world without God's healing. God's healing will give you vision to ensure you are doing good things and not bringing more harm to humanity. *"Your eye is the lamp of your body. When your eyes are healthy, your whole body also is full of light. But when they are unhealthy, your body also is full of darkness. See to it, then, that the light within you is not darkness." – Luke 11:34-35*

Allowing your light to shine means you have to work on improving yourself everyday.

Here are some Ways You can begin using to Improve Yourself in Just 10 Minutes or less

We use the word busy way too much. We say it when friends ask us how we are doing, as if being busy is an emotion. We use it as an excuse to procrastinate on unpleasant tasks. We use it to sound important at work, because being busy somehow equates to being successful.

But you're never too busy for 10 minutes, which is all it takes to improve yourself just a little each day. You can de-stress using meditation, yoga or reading. Track your unhealthy spending habits. Learn a new language. The possibilities are endless.

BIG TIP

Stop prioritizing the busy parts of your life and make time for the important things, such as the constant development of your mental, physical and emotional well-being.

For Your Body

1. Get moving

Committing to an hour-long daily gym routine or workout class can be overwhelming. It doesn't work with our schedule; there are more important things that can't be skipped. Try meditate walks with our Free Mindfulness Meditations on DrStem Be Encouraged YouTube Channel.

You get to relax and exercise.

2. Try Yoga

Yoga has long been shown to reduce stress and anxiety, and to improve overall well-being, but a survey conducted last year found that people who do yoga are 20 percent more likely to have a positive self-image. Give a quick daily routine a try using a free app such as Daily Yoga for guided positions.

3. Try a walking mindfulness meditation.

Quiet time for yourself can be powerful in helping reduce stress and invigorate your mind, but you might be hard-pressed to find a dark, calm, quiet room where you can get away. Get outside and combine nature with breathing exercises to rejuvenate your body and mind. Not sure how to walk and meditate at the same time? Follow these simple steps:

- As you begin to move, notice how your body feels. Does it feel heavy or light, stiff or relaxed? It's common to feel a little self-conscious at first, but the sensation will pass quickly.

- Next, start looking at what you see going on around you: the people, the trees, the billboards, the shop windows.

- Now, turn your attention to sounds. Don't get caught up in thinking about objects, just be aware of them as you pass by.

- Smell comes next. Note how the mind wants to create a story out of each smell.

- Notice any physical sensations. Perhaps it's the feeling of warm sunshine, the soles of your feet touching the ground, or your bad knee flaring up again, pay attention to feelings that come up. For instance, what happens when your rhythm is broken by a red light? And when the light turns green, do you speed up to pass that man on your left? Don't judge yourself—just notice your thoughts and let them go.

- Finally, shift your attention to your pace. Use the rhythm of your walking as a kind of home base—to come back to when you realize your mind has wandered. You'll find over time that something as routine as walking can transform into a tool you can use to relax, even as you go about your daily business.

- You also can walk using the mindful meditation on our YouTube Channel – DrStem Be Encouraged or search DrStem mindfulness meditation on YouTube.

4. Relieve back pain.

If you sit at a desk all day, perform a standing cat/camel stretch. Stand up and stretch every hour. I encourage others to take Breathing Breaks every hour set timer to get up stretch or walk around.

5. Take a Selfie to Keep not to share

No filters, no hashtags, just a selfie for you to enjoy and appreciate the things that make you uniquely you. After you take the selfie, write down three things you appreciate about yourself. Put them on your mirror to boost your confidence on days when you struggle with a negative self-image. This is my favorite my phone has thousands of selfies, LOL

6. Fight off Emotional Enemies

Find ways to combat daily emotional stressors, including worrying, anxiety and depression. Check out our App and websites www.drstemmie.com . We also conduct two workshops a month for Women Self Care and Success which you might enjoy as we address mental health, wellness, success, careers and business needs. Learn more at: www.womenempowermentworkshops.com

7. Take a guilt free nap

Dragging in the afternoon? Skip the cup of coffee or burst of sugar. Just 10 minutes of shut-eye can dramatically improve your clarity, alertness and accuracy. This works 10-30 minutes even better.

8. Find yourself a cheerleader

A study published in the Journal of the International Association for Relationship Research found that participants who surrounded themselves with people who were exposed to positive messages about their bodies were more likely to stabilize or lose weight. Enlist an uplifting friend to take a daily 10-minute walk with you, even if its talking to your friend on the phone while walking that works too.

9. Sip on a red.

Red wine might help lower the risk of heart disease and stroke. So go ahead and pop the cork.

For Your Wallet

10. Check your Credit score

In a survey of more than 2,000 U.S. adults, only 9 percent of participants knew that you can have more than three different credit scores. Your credit score is tabulated based on nearly 100 different sources and can be affected by your daily financial habits. Keep tabs on your credit score using free online resources.

If you are in the USA I use www.CreditKarma.com.

11. Track Your Spending

After a long weekend with friends, there is always an element of guilt when you look at your bank account to see the damage. On Monday morning, we all promise ourselves that we'll spend less money on frivolous things. We start tracking every purchase to try to stay accountable. But that can be overwhelming. Start by tracking your three biggest problem areas, and zero in on those.

12. Indulge

Having a budget is smart and staying accountable is a necessary aspect of smart financial strategies. But don't get so caught up in tracking finances that you forget to live a little. Take a break from the budget and splurge on your favorite snack or dessert. Find a quiet spot outside and cherish the moment of treating yourself.

13. Learn From Others

Read one financial blog post per day and learn from people who have already made the money mistakes you're making right now. Popular blogs such as Get Rich Slowly and Money Crashers offer advice on everything from investing to car insurance discounts.

For Your Emotional Well-Being

14. Seek Support

Life can be difficult. When money is tight, friends are unsupportive and work is draining, it's hard to stay positive and working toward goals. The problems aren't always major, but they can inhibit your ability to keep moving forward. Find support through online therapy programs or attend our monthly wellness workshops for more resources and support, at:

www.womenempowermentworkshops.com

15. Know Yourself

Knowledge precedes change. Start with understanding yourself. Grab our Self Love course at: https://www.drstemmie.com/loveyourself which has 13 week videos and audio chapters that have a wealth of information and guidance to self love and knowing about yourself.

16. Wake up for the sunrise.

And don't Instagram it! Sometimes it feels like we take pictures only to tally the number of likes, hearts and shares they will garner. Enjoy this beautiful moment for yourself.

17. Listen to Music

Listening to music can decrease your overall anxiety, stress and downward spiraling emotions. To me Music is Life. So grab a comfy spot and spend 8 minutes and 8 seconds getting your chill vibes on. Listen to any music you enjoy.

18. Have a giggle fest.

Indulge in a mini marathon of hilarious animal videos. Much like a quick meditation, laughing lowers stress and blood pressure and gives some sparkle to your frame of mind. Start by searching "Funny Cat Videos" and fall down the YouTube rabbit hole. You can also watch Netflix funny movies or watch movies on YouTube

19. Check in with yourself

When was the last time you asked yourself, how am I doing? And really listened? Ask yourself what's going right and wrong in your day. Too often, we exaggerate daily annoyances in our minds. By saying them aloud, we take away some of the power they hold over our mood.

20. Test your emotional intelligence

IQ, emotional intelligence is said to significantly affect our career success, relationships, communication skills and more. Discover your emotional strength and take any free IQ test to see where you are.

21. Put down your phone down

Did you know that we're all subjected to thousands of distractions throughout the day. A study published in the Journal of Experimental Psychology found that you can be distracted simply by hearing or feeling your phone vibrate, even if you don't pick it up. Try putting your phone out of sight (and touch) for 10 minutes of uninterrupted productivity. Give yourself a break

22. Practice Gratitude

Reminding yourself of the positive things in your life has staying power. Multiple studies point not only to sustained feelings of happiness but also a decreased number of physical ailments. Write down three to ten positive things every single day and take note of your increased mood.

23. Spread Love

Giving love to yourself others releases an increased level of oxytocin—the feel-good chemical—in our brains, which subsequently makes us feel more generous and happy. Don't have time to make it to a soup kitchen or charity drive especially during this covid? Try making a call or volunteering to making calls to those who are sick in your church or any church.

That is a great feeling? Any other charities you can reach would also be great.

24. Dismiss worrisome thoughts

Losing sleep over a fight you had with your spouse, a friend colleague? Well, if you don't have control over changing the situation change your response and find ways to stay calm and in good thoughts.

For Your Mind

25. Listen to the classics.

As your mom always said, they just don't make things like they used to. Take a step back through history by listening to classical audiobooks and you can listen to my free eBooks on YouTube search for DrStem eBooks for good ole encouragement and inspiration.

26. Take a break

Sometimes the best learning happens when we aren't learning at all. Give your brain a break by playing some of the most-loved games or watching shows, movies etc. OR Just Do-Nothing Rest Relax Replenish

27. Start a Life Handbook

Not a rule book, a to-do list or an action plan, but a book that forces you to reflect on where you were and envision where you want to go. It can be as simple as collecting your favorite quotes, inspirational photos and big dreams list. Grab a blank notebook and you're all set.

28. Read just One chapter

Just one. How hard can that be? Pause your Netflix binge session and commit to bettering yourself. I now have written over 40 books grab your favorite on amazon put Sithembile Mahlatini books or get a quick download eBook on www.womenselfcaresuccess.com

29. Learn a new word.

Expanding our vocabulary skills is a task we left in our third-grade classroom. We

know enough, and who wants to sound pretentious by throwing out words like eleemosynary instead of just saying charitable. But an extensive vocabulary does more than just make you sound smart. It allows you to better communicate your new idea to a group of investors or sell yourself in the interview of your dreams. Try using the Merriam-Webster dictionary app for a word of the day and use it 10 times in conversation.

30. Learn skills they didn't teach you in school

Problem-solving, decision making, leadership, time management—some of the things we wish we learned in college. Join our Women Empowerment Workshops monthly at www.womenemepowermentworkshops.com where we offer live and recorded workshops each month.

31. Become a Speed Reader

Trust me I didn't know either that this could be that much fun. Not every book requires you to read every word to reap the benefits. Train yourself to read faster and more efficiently using apps such as Spreeder that train you to read quickly without losing comprehension.

Set a goal between 50 and 5,000 words per minute and earn points as you progress.

32. Get cultural.

Don't have time to visit that new art exhibit? Don't have the resources to visit The National Gallery in London? Expand your knowledge of art with free apps and visit any country continent using Apps as well. So much fun and easier these days to visit anywhere you want to.

33. Learn a new language.

Duoliongo www.duolingo.com offers daily lessons in 21 languages in five- 10- or 20- minute increments.

34. Rediscover your childhood wonder.

First, buy The Book of Questions by Nobel Prize winner Pablo Neruda. Second, place it on your coffee table. Third, have a house party and unceremoniously ask questions such as, "Tell me, is the rose naked or is that her only dress?" LOL

For Your Career

35. Find a Coffee/Tea/Hangout Buddy

Most of the problems in our current life have already been experienced by people before us. Save yourself time and energy by asking a friend, colleague or mentor to take a quick coffee/Tea or hangout break. Ask them questions and really listen to what they have to say.

36. Welcome to the IVIES

Did you know Yale University offers free access to hundreds of courses recorded directly from real classrooms? Learn about capitalism from Douglas Rae, a political scientist and Yale University faculty member since 1974. Find the complete list of available courses from more than 10 universities on AcademicEarth.com or Udemy.com.

37. Use the 60/10 rule.

I know you are used to the 80/20 rule well there is the 60/10 rule as well. Work for 60 minutes and then do something for yourself for 10 minutes. Mindfulness expert Andy Puddicombe says, "The mind needs to be cared for, too. If it isn't given time to 'just be,' the consequences could decrease one's quality of life."

38. Scroll smarter.

Look for programs products that will enhance your health, life, career and business and look for what you need and take time to explore that first than clog yourself with many unused and unexplored programs and products.

39. Stick to Your Goals

Stay accountable by monitoring your good and bad habits. Stick to one project or one program at a time finish it then celebrate your accomplishment and move on user-friendly apps such as HabitBull offer daily, weekly and monthly progress reports that remind you to stay on track.

40. Get bored.

Turns out being bored actually boosts your creative juices. Take 10 minutes and do absolutely nothing. Let your mind wander and see where it takes you. I truly love doing this and believe I make sure I make this ME Time at lease three or more times a week, a time for absolutely NOTHING.

41. Write a letter to your future self.

What stories can you tell, what struggles did you overcome and what miracles came your way?

42. Say No. No is a complete sentence

Your time is your most valuable asset. Learn to say no and give yourself more time to do the things that make you smarter, better and happier.

43. Remember what you want

Sometimes we're so distracted by stresses that we never take time to settle down and listen to what our bodies and minds are telling us. Try this: Sit in a comfortable position, settle your breath, close your eyes, and as you breathe, mentally repeat the words I am for five minutes. Next, four times in a row, ask yourself What do I want? Don't feel like you have to answer it; let your mind settle down and see what bubbles up.

44. Question the status quo.

By doing this, you will be facilitating the skill of critical unlearning. What do you need to stop doing? What do you need to leave behind? What do you need to forget? What do you need to ignore? This is important if you want to grow and go forward, if you want to grow personally and professionally.

45. Challenge your assumptions.

Just because that's how we've always done it doesn't mean that we should keep doing it the same way. This can lead to the bias of experience, that the way we've done it is still the right way to do it. Go below the surface and discover the belief that is driving any behaviors that are not serving you. . What is the belief behind the habit or process(es) you were taught? Even if the belief is right, does it have a different application today? If it's valid, our commitment will go even deeper. If it's not, we might need to do some innovating.

46. Try something new.

This often leads to something better. Occasionally it comes through association with others. What seemed like an obstacle to progress became a breakthrough in efficiency. Sometimes it's as simple as trying an unfamiliar food or gaining unfamiliar knowledge..

47. Repurpose something old.

Sometimes the pearl gets lost in the process. The principle is good, but the delivery system is outdated. Don't miss the reliable because it's cluttered and camouflaged with irrelevance. This is more than recycling. It's also about ideas, attitudes, emotional intelligence, money, simplicity and wisdom.

48.. Connect with the bigger picture.

Synthesizing your life illuminates your path. Learning and growing is about capacity and skill. But it's also about connecting the dots. That is hard to do without knowing the bigger purpose of who we are and what we want. This takes learning to a whole new level. You are no longer just a teacher. You are a master teacher. Our program on Self Love is a great first step in setting up your Big Picture. Learn More at: https://www.drstemmie.com/loveyourself

49. Trust what you know.

- Trusting what you know gives you the courage to try new things. Here's what I know:
- The sun will come up tomorrow.
- What I am going through right now will pass.
- With one exception (you), the world is composed of other people.
- Be kind. Everyone I know is carrying something, going through something and overcoming something.
- The best things in life aren't things.
- People make honest genuine mistakes and others don't care
- You get out of life what you put in it.
- Gratitude is the healthiest emotion and outperforms gratification.

- What you focus on becomes your reality whether it's true or not.
- The quality of your life is dependent on the quality of your emotions.
- Bitterness is a downward spiral.
- I must actually have to forgive in order to live my life freely and fearlessly
- The only difference between a rut and a grave is the depth.
- I can change what I believe at any time
- I have the ability to change how I respond to life all the time
- All is well
- Everything is working out exactly as it supposed to in my life

50. Accept that You will repeatedly go through tough times and get back up again and again.

Tough times are a part of life especially for those who dream and do big things. They know that's how the world works and don't fight or complain about it, it is challenging for all of us and we just have to learn how to survive and make it work for us each time.

Without difficult times and failures, there is no learning, no growth. Those who shine their light and are successful know that nothing worth achieving comes without a struggle. They know there's a difference between suffering and struggling.

The Dalai Lama wrote, "Pain is inevitable. Suffering is optional Those who shine their light and are successful struggle and feel pain, but don't suffer because they are living their lives and pursuing goals that are in line with who they are, what they value, and what they believe to be their purpose or mission. To them, it is all worth it.

Will you embrace these 50 practical steps and allow your light to shine so bright that it blinds every nay Sayer and enemy around you?

To further encourage and empower you I have rounded up the best let your shine quotes, sayings, captions, status, to inspire you to be a good example and shine humbly to do good, and be good.

Let Your Light Shine Quotes

1. "The more light you allow within you the brighter the world you live in will be." – Shakti Gawain

2. "Simply shine your light on the road ahead, and you are helping others to see their way out of darkness."
   – Katrina Mayer

3. "Small lights have a way of being seen in a dark world."
   – Neal A. Maxwell

4. "You playing small doesn't serve the world. There's nothing enlightening about shrinking so others won't feel insecure around you. As you let your own light shine, you indirectly give others permission to do the same." – Marianne Williamson

5. "As we work to create light for others, we naturally light our own way." – Mary Anne Radmacher

6. "Do not allow others to diminish your light due to their own fears and insecurities. Instead, let your light shine so brightly, that you illuminate a pathway for others to find their way out of the darkness!"
   – Dr. Stacey A. Maxwell,

7. "Let your light shine today, and let your personality blossom, too. You don't have to be a people-pleaser, just a people-lover." – Beth Moore

8. "Your greatest test is when you are able to bless someone else while you are going through your own storm." – Unknown

7. "Forgiveness is my function as the light of the world." – A Course in Miracles

10. "Ours is the responsibility to keep our lights bright for others to see and follow." – Thomas S. Monson

11. "There is no darkness so dense, so menacing, or so difficult that it cannot be overcome by light."
– Vern P. Stanfill

12. "Nothing can dim the light that shines from within."
– Maya Angelou

13. "There are two ways of spreading light: to be the candle or the mirror that reflects it." – Edith Wharton

14. "We are told to let our light shine, and if it does, we won't need to tell anybody it does. Lighthouses don't fire cannons to call attention to the shining—they just shine." – Dwight L. Moody

15. "No one is useless in this world who lightens the burdens of another." – Charles Dickens

16. "The darkness around us might somewhat light up if we would first practice using the light we have in the place we are." – Henry S. Haskins

17. "Stars don't shine because they want to be seen. They shine because they are stars." – Alexander Den Heijer

18. "In the midst of darkness, light persists." – Mahatma Gandhi

19. "Your work is to discover who you are and then with all your heart give your light to the world."
– Jennifer Williamson

20. "If you want to give light to others you have to glow yourself." – Thomas S. Monson

21. "When you possess light within, you see it externally." – Anaïs Nin

22. "Your only obligation in any lifetime is to be true to yourself." – Richard Bach

23. "Be aware that who you are and what you have to offer can be a beacon to some lost soul." – Iyanla Vanzant

24. "I wish I could show you when you are lonely or in darkness, the astonishing light of your own being." – Hafiz

25. "Accept your light and let it shine to create your own lighthouse on a stormy night."
– Pauline Duncan-Thrasher

26. Light can shine without the presence of darkness, but through darkness light shines brighter with belief, confidence and more resilience. - DrStem

27. "Let your beautiful light shine."

28. "Shine your light and let the whole world see."

29. "She sparkles because she believes." – Kailin Gow

30. "Positive energy makes a person shine from within."

31. "Let not discouraging feedback dim your brightness."

32. "A person always shines when he has a strong desire."

33. "Unless you glow the world cannot see your presence."

34. "Smile, let your inner light shine." – Lailah Gifty Akita

35. "The shine in you starts vanishing as you start giving up."

36. "The beauty is not in the glowing skin but the shining soul."

37. "Make today amazing and let your light shine!" –
- Stacia Pierce

38. "The hope of sparks comes from within and lights up the outside."

39. "Don't be afraid to shine. The world needs your light." – Timi Nadela

27. "Let your beautiful light shine."

28. "Shine your light and let the whole world see."

29. "She sparkles because she believes." – Kailin Gow

30. "Positive energy makes a person shine from within."

31. "Let not discouraging feedback dim your brightness."

32. "A person always shines when he has a strong desire."

33. "Unless you glow the world cannot see your presence."

34. "Smile, let your inner light shine." – Lailah Gifty Akita

35. "The shine in you starts vanishing as you start giving up."

36. "The beauty is not in the glowing skin but the shining soul."

37. "Make today amazing and let your light shine!" – Stacia Pierce

38. "The hope of sparks comes from within and lights up the outside."

39. "Don't be afraid to shine. The world needs your light." – Timi Nadel

40. "The ones who got your back should be the ones shining in your eyes."

41. "Let the darkness be a chance to shine your inner light." – Avina Celeste

42. "Small lights have a way of being seen in a dark world." – Neal A. Maxwell

43. "Lanterns burn bright but people who oblige to help others burn brighter."

44. "The distance between your dream and reality is called action." – Unknown

45. "As we let our light shine, we unconsciously give other people permission to do the same." – Nelson Mandela

46. "Give it all you've got and you'll shine like you didn't even think you would."

47. "I do most of my work sitting down; that's where I shine." – Robert Benchley

48. "Be fearless, because the world needs what you have to give." – Eileen Anglin

49. "The similarity between a human and a torch is that both need a push to glow."

50. "Fools close their eyes and think that no one is watching, their shine fades away."

51. "If you want to give light to others you have to glow yourself." – Thomas S. Monson

52. "If you have the power to make people agree with you then you're already shining."

53. "And like a colorful bloom of temporary lights in the sky, you will shine." – Chad Sugg

54. "It's that heart of gold and stardust shine that makes you beautiful." – R.M. Broderick

55. "You don't wait for the brightness to shine on you, instead, you go towards it and find it."

56. "Standing with others means following the crowd, standing out alone is when you shine."

57. "It is only those who believe in their ability who shine when it matters." – Maurice Greene

58. "Glitter is attractive because it shines, similarly, a shining human seems attractive instantly."

59. "Brighten your Love Light, allow your inner glow to reveal itself to the world." – Ruth Soltman

60. "Let your light shine so brightly that others can see their way out of the dark." – Katrina Mayer

61. "The more light you allow within you the brighter the world you live in will be." – Shakti Gawain

62. "Know what sparks the light in you. Then use that light to illuminate the world." –Oprah Winfrey

63. "The humans who are energetic and happy release positive energy so does a diamond that sparkles."

64. "Ours is the responsibility to keep our lights bright for others to see and follow." – Thomas S. Monson

65. "There are two ways of spreading light: to be the candle or the mirror that reflects it." – Edith Wharton

66. "You shine today, tomorrow it will be someone else, this continues till there is brightness everywhere."

67. "Your greatest test is when you are able to bless someone else while you are going through your own storm."

68. "Stars don't shine because they want to be seen. They shine because they are stars." – Alexander Den Heijer

67. "You may think your light is small, but it can make a big difference in other people's lives. Let your light shine."

70. "I preach darkness. I don't inspire hope—only shadows. It's up to you to find the light in my words."
– Charles Lee

71. "You can overcome whatever is going on around you if you believe in the light that lives within you."
– Justine Edward

72. "Let your light shine. Shine within you so that it can shine on someone else. Let your light shine."
–Oprah Winfrey

73. "Remember diamonds are created under pressure so hold on, it will be your time to shine soon."
– Sope Agbelusi

74. "Let your light shine. Be a source of strength and courage. Share your wisdom. Radiate love."
– Wilfred Peterson

75. "I don't think that people don't succeed; I think that it takes time! Everyone will have their time to shine!"
– JoJo Siwa

76. "Your work is to discover who you are and then with all your heart give your light to the world."
– Jennifer Williamson

77. "Simply shine your light on the road ahead, and you are helping others to see their way out of the darkness." – Katrina Mayer

78. "You are the star in the sky, shine your light on the path of others on your dark days to let them know who you are." – Lord Robin

79. "How much you downfall a genius, he will outshine all and how much you uplift a fool, he will not shine at all." – P.S. Jagadeesh Kumar

80. "Let your light shine today, and let your personality blossom, too. You don't have to be a people-pleaser, just a people-lover." – Beth Moore

81. "You truly are as bright, vibrant and warm as the light shinning down on you. You just have to believe and let your light shine." – Jennifer Gayle

82. "Shine bright. We are each the star of our own life...we get to decide who is in our life and where it goes...never let anyone take your leading role away."

83. "When pain brings you down, don't be silly, don't close your eyes and cry, you just might be in the best position to see the sun shine." – Alanis Morissette

84. "Miracle in your life is like the one-sided bright moon facing the earth, on the other side your sacrifices and struggles faced to shines." – Dr.P.S. Jagadeesh Kumar

85. "The most fascinating people, those who made a mark on this Earth, who changed history and culture are always those who were a little different."
– Eileen Anglin

86. "Do not shrink your beautiful light to make someone else feel more comfortable. Be who you are without hesitation and you will inspire others to shine, too!"
– Unknown

87. "You have come from His presence to live on this earth for a season, to reflect the Savior's love and teachings, and to bravely let your light shine for all to see."
– Thomas S. Monson

88. "You must be an artist and a citizen of the world. You must speak to this stuff that's happening. You must do what you can to shine a light on it, help people through it." – Leslie Odom, Jr.

89. "You are on a soulful path that asks you to step into the greatest version of yourself. It is a sacred gift to shine your brightest light, not just in your moments of glory, but each day." – Debbie Ford

90. "Try not to get lost in comparing yourself to others. Discover your gifts and let them shine! Soft ball is amazing that way as a sport. Everyone on the field has a slightly different ability that makes them perfect for their position." – Jennie Finch

91. "You are the light of the world. A town built on a hill cannot be hidden neither do people light a lamp and put it under a bowl. Instead they put it on its stand and it gives light to everyone in the house. In the same way let your light shine before others." – Unknown

SHINE YOUR LIGHT QUOTES

In the midst of darkness shine your soul like a guiding star to everyone around. Believe in yourself and do what is right. Courage and confidence with a pure heart and mind can be really life changing.

1. "If you want to shine you need to light up."

1. "Do not try to shine by someone else's influence."

2. "Stars prove that you can shine even in the dark."

3. "We stand in the dark and expect the world to see us shine."

4. "In the midst of darkness, light persists."
   – Mahatma Gandhi

5. "Without darkness, nothing could be able to shine glamorously."

6. "A soul is always shining underneath, the body has to express it."

7. "You shine to prove yourself not because someone expects you to."

8. "When you possess light within, you see it externally."
   – Anaïs Nin

9. "The shine in you should not decrease for the sake of someone else."

10. "Nothing can dim the light that shines from within."
    –   aya Angelou

11. "Count on me to shine where it doesn't count."
    – Katya Zamolodchikova

12. "Be the moon that shines even in the dark when people cannot see the path."

13. "If you want to shine like a sun, first burn like a sun."
    – A. P. J. Abdul Kalam

14. "Forgiveness is my function as the light of the world."
    – A Course in Miracles

15. "Your only obligation in any lifetime is to be true to yourself." – Richard Bach

16. "If I could be granted a wish, I'd shine in your eye like a jewel." – Bette Midler

17. "No one is useless in this world who lightens the burdens of another." – Charles Dickens

18. "Like a single candle can light the whole room a single human can light a whole society."

19. "Look, I can't dim my shine just because some people feel uncomfortable." – Israel Adesanya

20. "As we work to create light for others, we naturally light our own way." – Mary Anne Radmacher

21. "Look after yourself from within, and your beauty will shine through on your skin." – Shanina Shaik

22. "I'm very much about letting other people shine, because it makes us all shine brighter."
– Chelsea Handler

23. "Be aware that who you are and what you have to offer can be a beacon to some lost soul." – Iyanla Vanzant

24. "Your greatest test is when you are able to bless someone else while you are going through your own storm."

25. "An evil person is like a dirty window, they never let the light shine through." – William Makepeace Thackeray

26. "I wish I could show you when you are lonely or in darkness, the astonishing light of your own being."
– Hafiz

27. "Accept your light and let it shine to create your own lighthouse on a stormy night." – Pauline Duncan-Thrasher

28. "You make up a character, there's always gonna be parts of you that, like it or not, shine through."
– Taika Waititi

29. "There is no darkness so dense, so menacing, or so difficult that it cannot be overcome by light."
– Vern P. Stanfill

30. "An age is called Dark not because the light fails to shine, but because people refuse to see it."
– James A. Michener

31. "My emotions kind of shine through my face, so whatever I'm thinking is what I'm portraying as well."
– Laurie Hernandez

32. "We do not seek to impose our way of life on anyone, but rather to let it shine as an example for everyone to follow." – Donald Trump

33. "The darkness around us might somewhat light up if we would first practice using the light we have in the place we are." – Henry S. Haskins

34. "Beset by a difficult problem? Now is your chance to shine. Pick yourself up, get to work and get triumphantly through it." – Ralph Marston

35. "Better to illuminate than merely to shine, to deliver to others contemplated truths than merely to contemplate." – Thomas Aquinas

36. "Bid, then, the tender light of faith to shine By which alone the mortal heart is led Unto the thinking of the thought divine." – George Santayana

37. "There is someplace where your specialties can shine. Somewhere that difference can be expressed. It's up to you to find it, and you can." – David Viscott

38. "Appreciation is the highest form of prayer, for it acknowledges the presence of good wherever you shine the light of your thankful thoughts." – Alan Cohen

39. "Being a star just means that you just find your own special place, and that you shine where you are. To me, that's what being a star means." – Dolly Parton

40. "Choose to be kind. Choose to forgive. Let your love grow and shine so that people may look at the example of your life and glorify God in Heaven."
– Victoria Osteen

41. "Part of my role and part of my job is to shine a spotlight on issues that need that spotlight, whether it's people, whether it's causes, issues, whatever it is."
– Prince Harry

42. "We are told to let our light shine, and if it does, we won't need to tell anybody it does. Lighthouses don't fire cannons to call attention to the shining—they just shine." – Dwight L. Moody

43. "Everybody has fallen down or been disappointed in love. Where you truly shine is when you get back up. Use it as a learning experience and believe in all of the possibilities." – Sherry Argov

44. "People are like stained-glass windows. They sparkle and shine when the sun is out, but when the darkness sets in, their true beauty is revealed only if there is a light from within." – Elisabeth Kubler-Ross

45. "People just see the shine. They don't see the grind, the bags under my eyes. It was a lot of grinding, setbacks… I ain't finna let nothing stop me. Wherever I stop at, I already know who I am." – Kodak Black

46. "I've spent a lot of my life forcing myself to do the right thing, and nowadays, I've just forgotten about all that. It's far more romantic just to let all your vices and fetishes come out and shine." – Kevin Parker

47. "Do not allow others to diminish your light due to their own fears and insecurities. Instead, let your light shine so brightly, that you illuminate a pathway for others to find their way out of the darkness!"
– Dr. Stacey A. Maxwell

48. "Enthusiasm is the yeast that makes your hopes shine to the stars. Enthusiasm is the sparkle in your eyes, the swing in your gait. The grip of your hand, the irresistible surge of will and energy to execute your ideas." – Henry Ford

49. "You playing small doesn't serve the world. There's nothing enlightening about shrinking so others won't feel insecure around you. As you let your own light shine, you indirectly give others permission to do the same." – Marianne Williamson

LET YOUR LIGHT SHINE QUOTES FROM THE BIBLE

There's nothing enlightening I grew up in Zimbabwe, where my mother didn't play, we all had to attend church and Sunday school. I am very proud of this upbringing and humble beginnings. My very, very, favorite song was this little light of mine, I'm gonna let it shine, let it shine, let it shine.

This is also the very reason why I had started writing my book, Let Your Light Shine way before the pandemic because that was my prayer and drive when times became tougher than my inner and outer strength.

I hope you enjoy these let your light shine quotes from the Big Book, the best manual ever with every guidance of our next best step.

Let Your Light Shine So Bright that it quietens even your own self-doubt. DrStem

1. "Let your light shine." – Matthew 5:16

2. "The Lord is my light and my salvation." – Psalm 27:1

3. "Your word is a lamp to my feet and a light to my path." – Psalm 119:105 ESV

4. "The light shines in the darkness, and the darkness has not overcome it." – John 1:5

5. "For at one time you were darkness, but now you are light in the Lord. Walk as children of light."
– Ephesians 5

6. "Let your light so shine before men, that they may see your good works, and glorify your Father which is in heaven." – Matthew 5:16

7. "You are the light of the world. A city set on a hill cannot be hidden. Your word is a lamp for my feet, a light on my path." – Matthew 5:14

8. "'The people living in darkness have seen a great light; on those living in the land of the shadow of death a light has dawned." – Matthew 4:16

9. "God requires his people to shine as lights in the world. It is not merely the ministers who are required to do this, but every disciple of Christ. Their conversation should be heavenly." – Ellen G. White

10. "Men are not born saints with special gifts and privileges. They fight against the world, the flesh and the devil, and as they conquer, the spirit of Jesus begins to shine through with more clarity." – Mother Angelica

11. "It is still breathtaking to me to watch people bring love, preciousness and kindness to their inner world,

allowing the light of God to shine through their eyes so that the beauty of their soul can come forth."
– Debbie Ford

Self Love Affirmations

To Let your light shine you will need to encourage yourself everyday. The following positive statements will be very helpful. pick one or two a day and write the statement in your journal then read that out loud to yourself throughout the day.

With self love affirmations, the goal is that by repeating them, you promote love for the self, which you then have available to give to anyone you pass.

Here are a few of my favorites:

1 - I deserve to be happy

2 - I did my best to love myself so far today

3 - I am always receiving the answers I need on my path

4 - I am open to love coming in from the Universe around me today

5 - I love my ability to persevere through challenges

6 - I appreciate my body's ability to keep blood flowing

7 - I appreciate the color of my eyes and skin

8 - I love that it is easy for me to spot the silver lining in any situation

9 - I am helpful to others in just the right way

10 - I am always learning new things

11 - I am providing safety to myself today

12 - I love my ability to soak up the knowledge and insight around me

13 - I'm a smart person with a worthy place in this world

14 - I have something to offer everyone I meet

15 - I speak lovingly to those around me

16 - I am safe where I am right now

17 - I am cared for and protected by me

18 - I am free to honor myself first today

19 - I acknowledge the loving acts I do for others

20 I love my body and all it does for me

21. I am enough

22. I am worthy of love

23. I respect my own boundaries

24. Today, I choose me

25. I love the woman/man that I am

26. I am loved

27. I am deserving of love

28. I am kind to myself

29. Love flows from within me

30. I am beautiful, inside and out

31. I embrace my unique individuality

32. I deserve happiness

33. I let go of negative self talk

34. I am whole

35. Everything I need is within me

36. I am in control of my happiness

37. I am capable of reaching my goals

38. I accept myself unconditionally

39. I do not let my fears hold me back

40. I am grateful for all that I have

41. I make time to care for myself

42. I love and accept all of me

43. Loving myself comes easily and naturally

44. I am strong and resilient

45. I am successful

46. My capacity for love is infinite

47. I let go of those who do not have my best interests at heart

48. I let go of my past and live in the present

49. I am growing each and every day

50. I forgive myself and learn from my mistakes

51. I am a work of art

52. I am valued

53. I allow myself to feel deeply

54. I am open to receive love

55. I love the body I was born with

56. I can achieve anything I set my mind to

37. I overcome challenges with grace and ease

58. I have a warm and caring heart

59. I am exactly who I need to be in this moment

60. I send love to my fears and doubts

61. I deflect negativity

62. I believe in myself

63. I can say no when something does not serve me

64. I let go of that which no longer serves me

65. I accept compliments easily

66. I release any need for suffering

67. I have a lot to offer the world

68. I love every part of what makes me who I am

69. I am blanketed in the Universes' loving energy

70. My life is filled with love and joy

71. I have always and will always try my best

72. I have achieved great things

73. I respect myself

74. My life is a place of balance and harmony

75. I have the power to change my world

76. I choose to stop apologizing for being me

77. I am not my mistakes or my flaws

78. Others accept and love me for who I am

79. I prioritize myself and my needs

80. I radiate confidence

81. My mind is filled with loving thoughts

82. I attract positive and loving people into my life

83. The more I practice loving myself, the more lovable I become

84. I let love in

85. I let my love for myself increase each day

86. Love flows freely from inside of me

87. I practice self-compassion when I do not succeed

68. I honor my own life path

89. I honor and respect my limitations

90. I have so much to love about myself

91. My life is a reflection of the love inside me

92. The only approval I need is my own

93. I radiate love

94. I love my own company

95. I do not need anyone to feel worthy

96. I attract love and light

97. I release the need to judge myself negatively

98. Today I start loving myself more

99. I am capable of loving fully and completely

100. I treat my body with love and care

101. I am powerful and confident

102. I trust in my ability to make it through difficult times

103. I trust my intuition

104. My life is full of endless opportunities for success and happiness

105. My inner world creates my outer world

106. I reward myself for my hard work and dedication

107. I am balanced

108. The universe supports me, always

109. I have a loving relationship with my body

110. I can choose self-love whenever I desire

111. Loving myself means I am able to love others more

112. I have a positive and healing effect on others

113. I have so much to celebrate in life

114. I am proud of myself

115. I choose to view my life positively

116. My body is my best friend

117. I choose to nourish my health

118. I am the healer of my own life

119. I am love

Life is all about endurance, persistence, strength, and embracing the change. When you adapt to change, improve every day and reinvent yourself it is easy to be the best version of yourself, allowing your light to shine.

Feel free to share these uplifting quotes with friends and family

More Ebook Resources are on our website www.womensuccessselfcare.com and more audio resources on the DrStem Be Encouraged channel on YouTube.

Don't forget to sing along:

This little light of mine, I am going to let it shine, will you let yours shine too?

Sing and Dance Until Your light Shines.

Let your Light Shine!!!

This Little Light of Mine Lyrics

1   This little light of mine,
    I'm gonna let it shine.
    This little light of mine,
    I'm gonna let it shine.
    This little light of mine,
    I'm gonna let it shine,
    let it shine, let it shine, oh let it shine.

2   Ev'rywhere I go,
    I'm gonna let it shine.
    Ev'rywhere I go,
    I'm gonna let it shine.
    Ev'rywhere I go,
    I'm gonna let it shine,
    let it shine, let it shine, oh let it shine.

3   Jesus gave it to me,
    I'm gonna let it shine.
    Jesus gave it to me,
    I'm gonna let it shine.
    Jesus gave it to me,
    I'm gonna let it shine,
    let it shine, let it shine, oh let it shine.

Grab Your Copy on Amazon or eBook from www.womenselfcaresuccess.com ; www.drstemmie.com and www.womenempowermentworkshops.com

Learn More about this video and audio self-paced Course at https://www.drstemmie.com/loveyourself

DrStem Books and eBooks

eBOOKs now available at www.drstemmie.com under **"Empowerment Books"** tab and also available on Etsy www.womenselfcaresuccess.com

These Books are available on **AMAZON** and Book Stores near you.

CONTACTS- Resources

"Self-Care Workshops Relaxation"
Join Our Memberships to Attend All Our Weekly Workshops For Free or Pay as You Go for each Workshop.

For more information, including workshop topics and dates, visit her website at www.drstemmie.com

One on Once Coaching
For one-on-one Life, Business, Career, Relationship Coaching, please call 781 (254-1602) or email info@drstemmie.com or drstem14@gmail.com for more information.

Digital Courses and E Books
Visit our website www.drstemmie.com and go to **Digital Courses** tab, then the *"Women Empowerment"* tab
https://www.drstemmie.com/empowermentebooks

For Teens, please follow the *"Parent-Teen"* tab:
https://www.drstemmie.com/parentsteensebooks

Bounce Back Better Empowerment Conference
Join us every December for this uplifting, motivating, inspiring, encouraging Virtual Conference until it is safe to meet in person. More info available on our website: www.drstemmie.com

Bounce Back Better Apparel

Visit: https://bouncebackbetterapparel.com/

Women Self-Care Success Store

Visit: https://www.womenselfcaresuccess.com/

DrStem Radio/TV Show & Podcast

Listen on our platform www.InspiredChoices.ca

On Spotify and everywhere you listen to your Podcasts, You Tube, or on Facebook.

Speaker, Trainer

To Book Dr Stem as a Speaker or Wellness, Corporate Trainer please email us at: info@drstemmie.com

Download Corporate Brochure at:

https://www.drstemmie.com/Global-Training-Coaching-&-Consulting-Services-Inc

ABOUT THE AUTHOR

Dr Stem Sithembile Mahlatini (Life Plus) is an inspiring Coach, Speaker, Trainer and Author. Her passion is Empowering Others through her work as a Motivational Speaker, Author, Coach, Personal and Professional Development Trainer, and Workshop Facilitator. She is also a mindset, and confidence coach for women.

As a Coach, she helps women become crystal clear and successful in their business, work, and life by overcoming fear, self-sabotage, the imposter syndrome, stress, and procrastination.

As a Trainer, her work is focused on wellness, personal and professional development. Some of her popular training includes: Leadership Mindfulness; Compassion Fatigue and Stress Management and The Emotional Toll of the Pandemic-Supporting Your Employee's Mental Health.

Her life goal and mission is to bring HOPE (that is Helping Other People Excel by living stress-free lives, pursuing their purpose and passion.)

Dr. Stem (Sithembile Mahlatini) was born and raised in

Zimbabwe, Africa, is the President and Founder of The Annual Bounce Back Better Empowerment Conference, The DrStem Empowerment Academy For Women Risers and Achievers at www.drstemmie.com, The Global Training, Coaching & Consulting Services, Inc, and a certified John Maxwell leadership Trainer.

Dr. Stem (Sithembile Mahlatini) is also an author of over 35 empowerment and inspirational books on her website www.drstemmie.com

Her books are also available on www.amazon.com.

Her Motto: *"We are not given a good life or a bad life. We are given a life. It's up to us to make it good or bad."*
- *Devika Fernando*

For God has not given us a spirit of fear, but of power, love, and self-control. **2 Timothy 1:7**

ABOUT THE EMPOWERMENT ACADEMY

The Empowerment Academy is a platform where women can have full access to life, career and business coaching, digital programs, eBooks, and tools for success in life, career and business with membership or individual bookings.

Corporations and Organizations can enjoy providing their employees with state-of-the-art wellness trainings, workshops, and digital programs. Trainings cover mental and health wellness, leaderships -Management skills, mindfulness, time management, organizational skills and more.

The Self-Care Workshops lift women up. The workshops are geared towards letting women know that they can be more, and each workshop provides them with the tools and the support to become more.

The Empowerment Academy provides all round real empowerment: with deep insight programs that address childhood issues, fears, mindfulness, stress management and success programs, with emphasis on an internal and positive change in each woman, so that she can find her passion, and purpose and change her life on her own terms.

THERE ARE TWO WOLVES INSIDE EACH OF US

ONE IS EVIL

ANGER
ENVY
SORROW
REGRET
GREED
ARROGANCE
SELF-PITY
GUILT
RESENTMENT
INFERIORITY
DECEPTION
FALSE PRIDE
SUPERIORITY
AND EGO

ONE IS GOOD

JOY
PEACE
HOPE
SERENITY
LOVE
HUMILITY
KINDNESS
PATIENCE
BENEVOLANCE
EMPATHY
GENEROSITY
TRUTH
COMPASSION
AND FAITH

Whichever WOLF wins is the one YOU feed most.

www.drstemmie.com

DR. STEM SITHEMBILE MAHLATINI

www.drstemmie.com

www.ingramcontent.com/pod-product-compliance
Lightning Source LLC
Chambersburg PA
CBHW070743060526
44119CB00071B/156